Advice

To My Son

Words of wisdom

to help guide you

through the journey of life

By

Sean

Leary

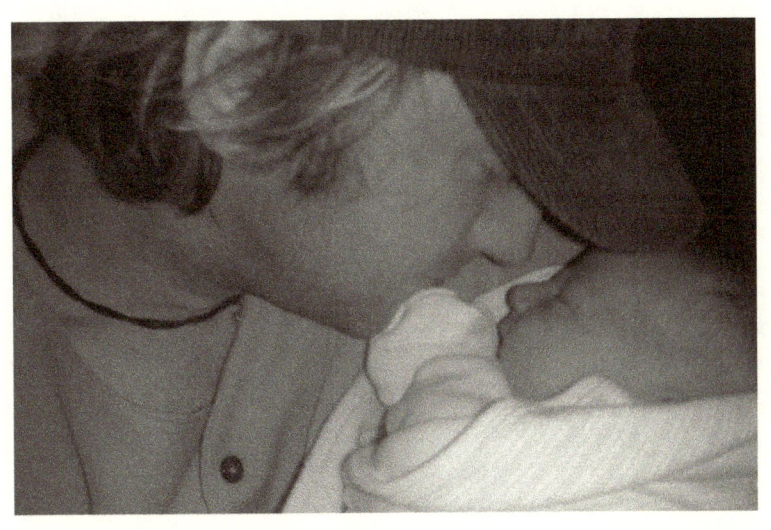

As always,

To Jackson

Advice To My Son is copyright 2017 Sean Leary. All material in this book is copyright 2017 Sean Leary. The name, trademark, and anything else of that ilk is copyright and trademark 2017 Sean Leary.

All rights reserved, including the right of reproduction in whole or in part in any form including book, eBook, audio, video, computer disc, CD-ROM, multimedia, Internet, and all other forms, whether yet known or developed.

Material within may not be republished or broadcast without the express permission of the author, unless in a promotional capacity. If used in a promotional capacity, all work within must be credited to the author and it must be noted that the work appeared in Advice To My Son, by Sean Leary.

This book is published in the United States by Dreaming World Books and Dreams Reach Productions.

ISBN # 978-0692230060

Library of Congress # Applied for.

Cover photo by Sean Leary. Interior illustrations and photos by Sean Leary and Jackson Leary.

Thank you to all my friends who have supported me and my work.

And as always, thank you to my son, Jackson, who is my guiding light in my creative pursuits and my world.

Introduction

This month, March 2017, my son, Jackson, will turn nine. His last year in single digits. Four years away from becoming a teenager.

As anyone who has been a parent can likewise attest, it's amazing how time flies. And even more amazing that no matter how old your children get, you still remember them, and there's still a spot in your heart, in which they're just born, little babies, blank slates with the world in front of them just waiting to be discovered.

As children, though, they're the same way. They've learned to walk, and talk, to draw and make art, to play sports and to write and read and do math, but they're still growing, still taking this crazy trip we all are through life, and still discovering new things.

And just as when they were just born, just as when they were toddlers, they need our guidance. They need our wisdom. They need our care and love.

My son is undeniably the best person I've ever had the honor of meeting, and I'm looking forward to continuing to experience the adventure of his life with him.

And as that time goes by, he may ask me for the advice I've gained in my years before him. Which is why I started writing advice to him shortly after he was born, and I've added to it every year on his birthday since then.

As I did, it meant more and more to him, as he realized exactly what it was that I was writing and how it pertained to his life.

And as I have shared this, others have reached out, people of all ages, to tell me how much it meant to them.

So many told me they wished they had a parent tell them these things.

Honestly, so do I.

I wish my mother and father had told me some of this when I was growing up. But they were from another time, another generation, when people weren't as open about these things, and certainly weren't as comfortable sharing their feelings or showing that they, too, were human beings capable of the failure from which wisdom is often gained.

I've tried to be that person to my son. I've tried to always be the parent I wish I had. The parent I hope will be the best for him, to help guide him on his journey and support him and love him, to help him feel strong and unconditionally loved.

To know I'll always believe in him, I'll always be there for him. Because I will.

I love you, son, and I hope you find this useful in your life's journey.

Always remember, no matter what, your Dad will always love you. Always…

And now, here are a few words of advice from your Dad…

Advice To My Son

Advice on...

Advice

Being a Person of Good Character

Being Happy

Being Optimistic

Getting Through Tough Times

Being Honest and Respectful

Being Unique and Following Your Own Path

Being a Rebel

Considering The Value And Worth of Things

Gifts To Give Yourself Every Christmas and New Year

Being a Good Parent

Working Hard and Succeeding

Surrounding Yourself With Good People

Being a Good Friend, Choosing Good Friends

Romantic Relationships

Growing and Evolving

Never Forget . . .

Happy to be with this fella again

On Advice . . .

There are people who love you who will give you advice.

Your Dad, for instance.

We're looking out for you. We love you. We're trying to help you.

But we aren't you, and ultimately, you have to make decisions for yourself.

When we, or anyone, gives you advice, think about what we're saying, why we're saying it, and how we're saying it.

When you were little, I told you not to goof around in the bathtub. I told you because I love you and I was looking out for you. I was afraid you might slip and hurt yourself. Well, one day you decided not to listen to your Dad and you were goofing around in the bathtub, and you slipped and your Dad had to rush you to the Emergency Room at the hospital for a few stitches in your chin.

Why was Dad telling you not to do something? Because I love you and I was trying to protect you. I told you about the potential consequences. I told you why I was doing it.

Consider that. Consider it wisdom well received when someone who loves you gives you advice and tells you because they want you to avoid pain or something negative. That's advice well listened to, and ultimately well taken.

A lot of the time, our advice comes from our own mistakes, our own pain, that we want you to avoid, because we love you and we want you to have a better life. And if I can impart that wisdom to you, to help you avoid the same mistakes I might have made, or to have you avoid mistakes I've seen others make, then you will live a happier life, and I will likewise be happier for you living that good life.

That's because my most important motivation is my love for you. I want to see you succeed, I want to see you happy, I want to see you have a wonderful life. I have no other motivation, no other ulterior motive. I am happy when you are happy, when you are healthy, when you are in a good place. That is the purest motivation you can find from anyone, and ideally you will find that from the people who love you and just want your happiness.

Not everyone is like that though, and so, whenever you get advice, you have to consider the source and the motivation.

It's a sad truth that not everyone is like that, not everyone will give you good advice. Some people will intentionally give you bad advice.

Some will be two-faced, and seem your friend to your face, but will not have your best intentions in mind. They will want to see you fail.

This is not because of you. This is because of them. It's not your fault, it's theirs.

Avoid those people at all costs. Keep them out of your life as much as you can, stay away from their toxic nature and do not take any of their advice, especially if it seems dubious.

There are other people who may not have ill feelings towards you, but their level of advice may vary between good and bad depending on their own judgement, attitude, experience, and way of seeing the world.

If you see someone who has made many bad decisions, and continues to do so, you might want to think about their advice before taking it. If they cannot learn from their mistakes, if they cannot make good decisions, they may not be able to give the greatest advice on how to do so.

In addition, consider the person's mood and their place in their life at the time they are giving their advice.

People's worldviews and attitudes tend to impinge upon their opinions. If someone is in an optimistic state, they'll tend to give more good and upbeat advice, and will tend to be more supportive of positive actions you might be taking. If they're in a pessimistic state, they'll tend to be more negative and cynical about both positive and negative actions.

Listen to people, but keep that in mind and add as much critical thinking as needed accordingly if someone with a pessimistic slant always seems to be shooting you down without good reason.

It's the same thing with getting criticism.

Criticism says as much about the critic as it does about what they're criticizing.

Some people will give you constructive criticism because they want you to improve, they want to look out for you, they want you to evolve and they're trying to help you, to show you ways in which you can improve. This is legitimate, and you should use this as advice to consider. Your father and other loved ones will try to do this. Some coaches and teachers and friends will do this. They want you to get better and them pointing out flaws is to make sure you recognize them so you can improve upon them.

Everyone is flawed. Everyone makes mistakes. There is no shame in being imperfect, for we all are. The difference is in how you deal with those mistakes and imperfections and how you strive to improve them and make them better. That's how we grow, that's how we evolve, that's how we get smarter or better at art or sports or anything in life, recognizing our weaknesses and working to make them better, to make them strengths.

But there are others, even some who will say they're giving you "constructive criticism," who are just criticizing you because they're trying to deflect attention or blame from themselves, because they're jealous or they resent you or because they just enjoy putting others down because it's easier than raising themselves up.

Criticism is just someone else's opinion.

Just like yours.

Nobody knows you better than yourself, so nobody else's opinion should matter as much on you as your own.

If someone criticizes you, think about who the person is, their motivation behind the criticism, whether they have your best interests in mind, whether they're a good person.

The opinions that should be most strongly considered are those of people who have proven themselves to be worthy of your trust, who you know love you and who you know have your best interests in mind.

Like your Dad.

I'm not perfect, nobody is, but I'll always have your best interests in mind. I'll always be looking to give you the best advice I can because I want to help you.

I love you, and I want you to have a great life, the best life you can.

Which is why I'm giving you this advice . . .

Being A Person Of Good Character

We are all the products of our environment and upbringing, with thousands of different factors along the paths of our lives weighing in on who we are. No two people are exactly alike, not even twins.

But one thing all of us can do is consider our actions and take responsibility for them, and try to do the right thing.

What is the right thing?

When you are considering your actions, considering your life, at the end of every day, if you can look in the mirror and honestly say you've done nothing to willingly hurt yourself and nothing to willingly hurt another human being, then you can be proud of yourself.

If you can further say that you've done things to make others' lives better, make the lives of your loved ones better and make your own life better, both short term and long term, then you have even more of which to be proud.

As always, remember, live in the present. If you string together enough good todays, you'll see that the tomorrows tend to be a lot easier.

Character is often defined by what you do when no one is looking. Anyone can make a big show out of doing nice things for people, to make themselves look good, but it takes someone of true character to do those same things for someone when no one will know but you and maybe the other person.

Be that person who is consistent in their character both when people are watching and when no one is.

We all make mistakes. Take responsibility when you do, but don't dwell on it and don't be too hard on yourself, especially if what you did was unintentional or an accident. Learn from your mistakes, take that wisdom, and move on.

We will all hurt other people. If you hurt someone unintentionally, or intentionally, apologize. Admit you were wrong, apologize for hurting them.

However, also recognize that sometimes people's feelings will be hurt by things you do or say because of their own things that they are sensitive to that others might not be. You may have no idea that someone is more sensitive to comments about their appearance or certain aspects of their being. You may try joking with someone or you may be seeing yourself as being lighthearted or not meaning anything personally, but they make take something you say or do a lot more seriously than you intended. If you inadvertently hurt their feelings due to this, apologize and move on.

And if they're the type of person that doesn't let you move on, then move on from them.

Don't let them use that against you or make you feel overly guilty, because they, like you, are imperfect and have hurt others as well. Don't let anyone use your mistakes against you, especially if you have sincerely apologized for them.

Admit your mistakes, apologize for them, learn your lessons from them, try not to repeat them, and then move on. Live your life.

Do what makes you happy. Let other people do what makes them happy. If neither of you are hurting anyone else, don't worry about it.

You might have blue hair. They might want to wear a shiny purple jacket with rainbow patterns and leopard stripes. They might want to play showtunes on the kazoo. You might think that soccer is the greatest sport ever invented. They might think that lacrosse is.

These are all personal preferences. There is no right, there is no wrong to them. And you shouldn't ever let anyone make you feel you're wrong or right for having them. You should never let anyone make you feel wrong for liking something when that something isn't hurting anyone else. Someone else may not like soccer or blue hair. Well, fair enough, they don't have to dye their hair blue or watch or play soccer. But they don't have any right to tell you that you can't, or to tell you you're wrong for doing either. And you shouldn't let them bother you or bother listening to them if they do.

Again, have no fear of moving on and away from people who ever make you feel bad for being you.

We live in a world of over six billion people at this point. The odds are, you will find other people who will accept you for who you are. You don't need people that do not accept you.

If someone makes you feel bad about yourself, about your life, about your choices, and you, your life and your choices are not hurting you or another person, then you need to move past that person making you feel guilty or feel bad for just pursuing your happiness.

Always remember that you have your family and loved ones who will always accept you, and your Dad, who will always love you no matter what.

People often project their fears or their insecurities or their angers on to other people rather than facing them themselves.

Maybe they're afraid that other people will make fun of them, or they're insecure about trying something new that they won't do well at.

The person who rolls their eyes at you for having blue hair might secretly wish they had the courage to dye their hair blue. Maybe they've always wanted to try something like that. But they're afraid. And there's a part of them that's jealous of you, that resents you, because you have the courage to do that.

But that's not really your fault.

That's theirs.

They have to overcome that, and it's not your responsibility to deal with that, nor should you ever let it impact you and your life and happiness.

Follow your own path. Follow your own happiness. If it's not hurting you, if it's not intentionally hurting anyone else, don't worry about what other people think.

You know yourself better than anyone else, so never let anyone get you down or bring you down due to their perception of you.

Again, if you've made a mistake, apologize for it, change your present and future behavior to reflect your contrition and evolution, and move on. Don't ever let anyone drag you back to your past because they can't get beyond it.

If, at the end of the day, you can honestly say you did not try to hurt yourself or others, and you honestly tried to be good to yourself and others, and you tried to live a good and positive life moving forward in strength, then that day is a success.

And if you have done that, if you have been a good person, regardless of who was or wasn't looking, then you will be a person of good character.

On Being Happy

If anyone ever asks you what you want to be when you grow up, or what you want to be in the future, tell them you want to be happy. If you're happy, everything else just kind of falls into place.

You will know what makes you happy.

Be honest with yourself.

You will know what makes your soul sing.

You will know what makes your heart bright.

You will know what makes you smile and laugh.

More than anyone else, you will know. And that is your bliss, your path, that you should follow. Know that I will always believe in you and always support you. What I want most for you is to see you happy. That brings me more joy than anything, and more than anything I wish you a very happy life.

There have been various times in my life when other people have tried to tell me what I should do. But I've done what I felt was best for myself, best for the people I loved, to best bring me and them happiness, because I knew what that was, and I knew that happiness was my goal.

Once you were born, I wanted to spend as much time with you as possible. So, I restructured my life and my priorities so I could do that. Because being with you, and experiencing as much of your life with you as I could, was most important.

Some people didn't understand that. They wondered why that was more important to me than money or recognition or awards or anything else.

Because to me, the greatest reward, the greatest treasure, was time spent with you.

I knew this.

I knew what made my soul sing.

I knew what made my heart happy.

That was time with you, that was being an active part of your life, that was being your Dad and being there for you, walking alongside you on this path of life.

And that's the path I followed.

So maybe I didn't have as high paying a job as I did before, or as I could have. Maybe I wasn't driving as impressive of a car, or having a lot of money to buy new clothes or shoes or whatever on a regular basis.

But none of those things carried any worth for me.

Happiness was the most valuable thing for me.

And my happiness was tied in with how much time I was able to spend with you.

It was more worth it for me to spend as much time with you as I could. Because those moments could never be replaced, could never be relived, could never be retrieved. Material things would come and go, but time, time, is something you can only spend once.

Time is something you can only spend once.

So make sure you spend it on the right things.

If you know what makes you happy, if you invest in that, then you will have invested your time and effort in a way you will never regret.

Laugh.

Be goofy.

Look around you for the beautiful things, the wonderful adventures, the things that make this world an amazing place.

Different foods, different music, different cultures, different stories, different art, different people and places and things. There are so many incredible things to discover, and each one offers the promise of new or renewed joy and wonder.

Be unafraid to enjoy life, to have fun, to be silly, to be a goofball, to just smile and laugh and be filled with joy, because that's really what it's all about.

There's a popular saying, laugh as if nobody is looking. I say, who cares if anyone is looking? Pursue your bliss. Laugh. Be happy.

Your life is not a democracy. Nor should it be. The public does not have a vote on what you do. Don't give it to them. Don't worry about what other people think. You decide what you do, what path you take and what happiness you pursue. If you are yourself, the right people will like you. The right people are those who like you for you, and who will not only accept you for who you are, but will like it, love it, and encourage you to be the best person you can be. Those are the people you should be around.

But what's most important is that you love yourself, is that you make yourself happy.

If you can make yourself laugh, you'll never be completely unhappy.

The best gift you can give yourself is your own love and friendship. You are a wonderful person and you have every right to be happy with yourself. If you can be, then you'll never truly be alone. You'll always have yourself to keep you company.

And always remember, your Dad loves you, believes in you, and will always be there for you.

Always remember at least one really, really funny movie quote or hilarious memory. Remember things that never fail to make you laugh or smile when you remember them.

Remember us playing with Thomas engines when you were little and making up little stories with them. Remember us sneaking into the Buffalo Bills football stadium. Remember us playing soccer and baseball in the front yard. Remember "Hey, I'm Goober!" Remember us traveling across the country and stopping at fun places along the way. Remember Every Saturday going to little engines and the comic book shop and getting pizza and going to the park. Remember Baby Bird, "tweet tweet." Remember "the first finger hugger" when you were born. Remember so many fun times and happy memories.

You'll need that.

There will be times when bad things happen. There will be times when you're sad. There will be times when you'll be down. That's just life.

But there are always good things in life as well.

And if you can remember them, if you can remember something, or several things, that make you laugh, those are incredibly valuable. When you're at your most down, they will remind you that life brings laughter as well.

Always remember, that no matter how sad you might be at any given time, life has the potential to bring great happiness too.

Always have wonderful memories to hold on to, to cherish, and to remind you of the beautiful things in life.

You have given me so many of those memories to hold on to. I hope I've given you enough of those good memories to last a lifetime as well.

What do I want you to be when you grow up?

I want you to have wonderful adventures, to have a fantastic life.

But above all, I want you to be happy.

On Being Optimistic

Ultimately, we have one choice between birth and death, and that's how we live our lives -- in optimism or pessimism, in faith or fear. You decide whether to be optimistic in this life. And that simple choice will make all the difference.

If you believe good things can happen, you will be right some of the time. If you work to make them happen, you will increase your odds.

Worrying or being pessimistic does nothing to help you.

It's one thing to think about potential complications and work to make sure they don't happen, but don't worry about the things you can't control.

Control what you can, work hard to make it the best for yourself and the people you love.

Don't worry about the rest.

Have faith, have faith in yourself, that no matter what happens, you will be good.

If you concentrate on what you do have, some of the time you may be unhappy. If you concentrate on what you don't have, almost all the time you'll be unhappy.

Try to live every day not as if it's your last, but as if it's your first and you want to start a really impressive streak of cool days.

You really never know what's going to happen. Sometimes the greatest things happen when you're not looking, and people or opportunities enter or re-enter your life in awesome and unexpected ways.

There are some people in life that are always optimistic, no matter what, and some people that are always pessimistic, no matter what. Always make sure that you surround yourself with as many of the optimistic and happy people as possible. It'll make all the difference.

Always look for the good in things and people, even if they're being jerks, because it's there, and often they're being jerks because they don't want you to find that good, or they're afraid to ever let it show.

But, that said, don't ever let people drag you down. They make their own decisions. If they want to decide to be down or negative, that's their choice, but you're better off being around people who are going to be upbeat. Everyone gets sad or depressed sometimes. We have things happen to us that make us sad, or make us depressed. But people who are negative for no reason or who are constantly looking for the bad in life are to be avoided. If you look for the bad, you can find it. But you know what? If you look for the good, you can find that too. I'd rather be around people who are looking for positive ways to get out of any bad spots and who are happy for the good things in their lives.

Every day when you look in the mirror take time to notice your positive attributes. Concentrate on them. Celebrate them. Allow them to take greater prominence than any negative things. Life is too short for you to make yourself unhappy.

Be your own best friend. Be good company to yourself. Enjoy your sense of humor. Make yourself laugh. Then you'll always be happy with your company and you'll never truly be alone. If you can be happy being by yourself, you won't have to allow substandard people into your life merely to stave off solitude. You can have higher standards and invite people into your life who will make it better.

We live in the present, working towards the future. If there's something in your past that will hurt you to remember it, then keep it in the past. You have control over bringing it into your present, and if it brings you pain, it doesn't belong in your life.

Don't ever let the sadness of the past prevent you from embracing the happiness of the future.

Good things can happen to anyone. But first you have to believe they can happen to you.

If you look for the good in life, you'll find it. If you look for the bad, you'll find that as well. The question is, which do you want to find, for that guides your journey and your destination.

You know how some people say if you don't have anything good to say, you shouldn't say anything at all?

Fair enough. That's good advice for the most part. If you have needless criticism, if you're not defending yourself or someone else, keep it to yourself.

But I think if you have something good to say you should say it. Nothing wrong with putting positivity out there, especially if it might make someone feel good about themselves.

Stay positive. Believe good things will happen to you.

Sometimes your heart makes a wish without your head being aware of it.

Funny how the universe tends to answer those more readily than when it's the other way around.

Good things are going to happen to you.

Good people are going to be in your life.

You are going to have a magnificent life.

Believe that.

Believe in you.

On Getting Through Tough Times

Everyone, everyone, everyone has tough times they need to get through.

Challenges are a normal part of life.

And getting through them makes us stronger.

You are a very strong boy. You have already faced many challenges in your life and I'm proud of how you have gotten through them, sometimes with help from your Dad, but sometimes all on your own. You are a strong person. You can get through tough times. I have faith in you. I believe in you. Always.

Remember that with challenges come opportunities and pathways to change.

Sometimes the reason you lose something is because it's going to be replaced by something better.

Sometimes fate saves you from what you think you want to make you available for what you need and what ultimately makes you happier.

But you don't see these things until later, when you can look at them in retrospect.

Have faith that those good things are going to arrive, because they will.

Don't worry. When tough times arrive, look at the situation with your head and your heart, think logically, think things through, put things into perspective.

Control what you can. Do what you can to make things right, to make things better.

If there is something you cannot control, don't worry about it. You can't do anything about it, and worrying will just make things worse.

Everything changes and all things pass. Don't let the bad times get you too down, don't let the good times slip by without appreciating them fully.

Always do something positive every day. Always do something to move forward. Even during the toughest, most difficult times in your life, you can find something positive to do.

The best way to build a great future is through the brick-by-brick construction of positive actions day after day.

Make lists of things you want to accomplish. Don't get too down on yourself if you don't accomplish them all. Be proud of the things you do accomplish. Be ambitious. Maybe you get some of them done, maybe it takes a while to accomplish others, but every day you take steps in a positive direction is a day in which you're moving towards a better life.

And always notice the good things around you.

Because there are always good things.

Beautiful things.

Beautiful people.

Wonderful music and food and art and books and films and scenery and little joys that are abundant in our world and are even more so within the infinite universe of your imagination.

If you fill your mind with good things, with positive things, even during tough times, you'll be amazed at how well your mood remains upbeat and optimistic.

When I have gone through tough times, I have made sure to constantly fill my life with good, with things I enjoyed, and I've looked for positive and beautiful things around me. I've looked at pictures of you and remembered happy times. I've listened to music I liked. I watched movies that made me laugh. I read books that made me think. I took walks and noticed the little, intricate, incredible worlds that are always around us, that we often don't notice in our constant rush. I looked up at the sky at night and during the day and thought of all the worlds out there yet to be discovered, and all the people, aliens just like me, on other worlds, wondering about the universe at the same time.

And I thought of times in my life when things were good and weren't so tough, and other times when things were tough, and how all those things passed, and that all tough times will pass too.

It really puts things into perspective.

The news will show you pictures of tragedies, but amidst those tragedies are good people helping other people through those difficult times.

The news will be full of stories about terrible people doing awful things. But think about how many people you know who are never in the news who do great things, nice things, positive things every day.

It's all a matter of perspective.

So, remember, even when things are at their toughest, there are good things around you for you to notice.

There is always beauty in this world if you just look for it.

And during the most difficult times, that's when you need to look for that beauty the most, because it will keep you happy, it will keep you optimistic, it will keep you going.

Sometimes life is a series of tough decisions. You just try to do what's right and try to do your best.

I'm not perfect by any means, but I always try to just do what's good and right, especially regarding decisions that impact you.

Don't be afraid to believe the good things people say about you. It may always seem easier for the bad things to stick, but both are opinions, so why not allow the good ones greater weight?

Remember, the people who really love you will be the ones who stick by you through the tough times.

The strongest bonds are forged when traveling on narrow paths.

Your true friends are the ones who stay by your side when the only thing you have to offer them is your friendship.

I will always be there for you, no matter what.

Everything will work out all right in the end. If it hasn't worked out yet, then it's probably not the end.

On Being Honest And Respectful

Honesty and respect are intertwined and they're both born of strength.

If you have inner strength and confidence, you will feel confident in being yourself and presenting your true self and your thoughts, feelings, and opinions to the world. And you won't need to worry about whether people agree, because you will be strong in your own convictions. Be strong. You are worthy of respect.

Respect that others have that same right. But recognize that you also deserve that respect.

It's ok to disagree with people. It's ok for them to disagree with you. You're going to disagree with yourself when you look back at some of the opinions and thoughts you had years ago that have changed. But be forthright. It's better for someone to honestly disagree than for either of you to have to lie.

Know the difference between a fact and an opinion. As much as possible, base your opinions on facts. Science is based in fact. Math. Other things that are provable and can be researched should be based on the facts as you can gather them. Make sure that when you have an opinion it is based upon factual evidence and truth. And recognize the difference between fact and belief. Anyone can believe anything. I can believe that the moon is made of swiss cheese and that giant space mice created the craters on it by nibbling it. But that doesn't make it true. Make sure you research the truth and know it as much as you can. It's ok to have opinions and beliefs, but recognize the difference between them and facts, and as much as possible, base your opinions on factual evidence. It will give them much more weight.

There are going to be some opinions that are completely subjective – your favorite food, your favorite music, your favorite sports teams, etc. – and recognize that there is no general wrong or right for those opinions. They're entirely opinions, one person's feeling. You have a right to your own preferences as do other people. Don't ever let anyone put you down for something that makes you happy. If you like a certain song or movie, that's fine if others don't like it, but they have no right to put you down for it. People will joke around but don't let people make you feel bad for something that makes you happy and brings you joy. Everyone has their own right to happiness. And respect that right in other people as well.

Make sure your actions follow your words. You aren't what you say you are, you are what you do. Actions need to follow words. The totality of both will help define your character.

Honesty and respect is really about sincerity and authenticity. It's about being secure in yourself and recognizing that you don't have to make everyone else happy. As long as you're not trying to hurt anyone else, you have the right to be who you are, you have the right to your own opinions and thoughts and feelings.

And so do other people. You either agree or you don't. And that's how you find your true friends. Those are the people that will accept you and love you for who you really are, when you show them who you really are.

You'll never know if people really like you or love you if you never show them the real you. And you will never know if you really like or love someone if they aren't honest and open with you.

If you're honest, you never have to try to remember what lie you told in order to keep up a façade. It's always better to just be yourself and be honest.

And if you're always yourself, people are going to like you for you, and you're going to know that.

It's better to be surrounded by people who like you for who you are than those who like you for who you're not, someone you're pretending to be. Likewise, it's better to be disliked by people for being yourself than liked when you're faking it.

And if someone is living a lie or habitually lies it's difficult to ever trust them, because you don't really know who they are.

The truth can be uncomfortable sometimes. But nobody should be that fearful of it if it is exposed. The truth most hurts those whose actions are deserving of contempt.

Now, that said, everyone keeps certain truths to themselves to spare the feelings of others. "Do I look fat in these pants?" is a trick question. Trust me. Be careful with that answer.

Those are occasions in which I would say prudent silence is your best option. Nobody is 100 percent honest 100 percent of the time. But we shouldn't lie about things that matter, things that are big and important, and we shouldn't go out of our way to be fake or to lie to people on a regular basis. And we especially shouldn't create a false and fake persona to make ourselves look better or to look like someone we are not.

It's too much effort to try to fake things and it's not worth it. If people don't like you for you, then those aren't your tribe, those aren't the people you're meant to be around.

It's too much effort. Just be yourself. The people who love you for that are the ones you're meant to be with.

Stand tall.

Stand tough.

Be yourself.

People show respect for you when you show respect for yourself.

And the best people are respectful of themselves and in turn respectful of others' rights to their own happiness and uniqueness.

It's never a bad thing to be a good, respectful person. In the end, you're the one who has to look at yourself in the mirror, and if you can say you did the right thing, you'll always be able to do that and smile.

It's ok to disagree with someone, but it doesn't have to be personal, it doesn't have to mean a giant battle. You can just agree to disagree.

If other people can't do that, then maybe those aren't the people you should be around or associate with in person or online. If someone always has to have their way, if they're too much effort and too much drama and they're too selfish then you should respectfully move on from them. It's not worth it. Invest your time in other people who are more mutually respectful of you as well.

Consider your actions before you take them. The best way to say you're sorry is to consider your actions before you commit to them and decide not to do hurtful things in the first place, so you won't have to apologize later.

Anyone can destroy, but it takes a greater person to create. And it takes a strong person to stand true to themselves and to their creations, not let others drag them down, and likewise respect other peoples' rights to do the same.

Again, you are never going to agree with everyone. There are always, always, always going to be people who disagree with you. So never bother trying to make everyone like you or agree with you. Just be yourself. Put your own feelings and opinions out there and stand behind them, stay strong.

Then the right people for you, the best people for you to be around, will know how to find you, and they'll know they can trust and respect you.

On Being Unique
And Following Your Own Path

Why waste time trying to fit in when you were born to stand out?

You are unique. You are the only you this world will ever have. You are the only person who can be the best version of yourself.

So why try being someone else? At best, you'll only be the second-best version of the original.

A visionary fires an arrow at a target no one else can see. A genius hits it. But neither draws the bow without the courage of their convictions. The journey of 1,000 miles does not begin with the first step. It begins with the thought of the first step and the conviction and courage to take it.

What's the point of thinking outside the box if you constantly remain inside the box? Why not just live outside the box? That way you can do all the thinking you want to, and enjoy a much better view.

No one knows you better than you, so why would you ever let the opinions of another person define you?

Don't be too stung by people's criticisms, especially if they just seem bitter or off-base. Oftentimes they say more about them than they do about you. Some unhappy people would always rather drag others down than make the greater effort of correcting their unhappiness.

Emulate good things you admire in others, but don't imitate those people. There's a reason you're unique. You're meant to bring something into this world that no one else can. If you're constantly trying to imitate someone else, you'll always be the second-best version of them rather than the best version of you.

When someone says you're "weird" it just means you don't meet that person's preconceived notion of what "normal" should be. Well, before you ever get down on yourself, look at the arbiter of that judgement and ask yourself if you want to fit in with that person's definition of "normal."

You don't. Don't let others define you. You define yourself.

And just because someone is different from you doesn't mean they're weird. It just means they're different. You can disagree with them, certainly. But we all follow different paths.

You're different from everyone else.

That doesn't make you weird.

That makes you unique.

That makes you beautiful.

On Being A Rebel

One of the purest forms of rebellion in this world is in following your own path and just being yourself.

No matter the trends.

No matter what other people think.

No matter what other people try to tell you is or isn't popular.

Do what you want.

Take the path you want.

As long as it's not hurting anyone else, as long as it's not hurting you, as long as it's making you happy, do it.

Another form of rebellion is in in refusing to let others' actions towards you dictate your behavior towards them.

Follow your own path.

Always.

You want to really be a rebel? Don't do what everyone else thinks is "cool." Don't follow the brainwashing and the cookie cutter path of what society says is supposed to be "cool." Don't look to the media or entertainment and their cliché nihilism and tawdry glorification of insipid self-destruction and prescribed "cool."

Advertising companies and commercials and businesses will try to brainwash you. They need to brainwash you into buying whatever it is they're selling so that they can keep making money. And they brainwash people by making them feel bad about themselves. They brainwash people by making them feel bad about themselves and then by making them think that whatever they're selling is the solution to their problem, that whatever they're selling is what will somehow make them feel better, will make them cool, will help them fit in, will help people love them.

That's a bunch of malarkey.

Don't fall for it.

You're better than that.

You're better than them.

They're going to try to brainwash you into thinking whatever they're selling is something cool, or something you need to be cool, to fit in.

But nobody needs anything else to be cool.

All they need is themselves.

And all they need is to find the right people who will love them for themselves.

That's the coolest thing.

Finding your tribe.

Finding your people.

Where you can be yourself, and they can be themselves, and you accept each other.

But that confidence is sometimes in short supply among people, because we live in a society where people are constantly bombarded by advertising and messages that they aren't good enough.

So, people think they aren't good enough.

That's why the coolest thing is confidence.

The coolest thing, the thing that will make you most happy and that, ironically, will most draw people to you, is the courage inside that you are happy with just being yourself.

People will be drawn to that confidence, to that happiness, because they want to have it themselves. And they want to just be themselves, and they want people to accept them for that.

The only place you need to fit in is with yourself. At the end of the day, you will realize that you are the only person you are with all the time. And you are the person you need to be happy with at the end of the day.

Just be yourself. That's enough. That will be enough to the people who are worthy of being your friends. That's always enough for me. I love you for who you are, because you are the most incredible person I have ever met.

Believe that. Believe in yourself. See yourself and all your wonder as I see you. Because I love you. I believe in you.

And I know you better than anyone except yourself, because I've known you since you were born and spent more time with you than anyone else. I've seen you in countless ways and in all ways you are the most beautiful, amazing person I have encountered.

In a world of selfishness, narcissism, and rudeness, where people are taught to believe that standoffishness and needless negativity is "cool," rebel by being positive. Rebel by being nice. Rebel by being upbeat and happy.

Have manners. Be polite. Be a gentleman.

Give a sincere, appropriate compliment.

Do random acts of kindness or nice things for people without expecting anything in return, solely because it will make someone's life better.

Bring happiness to someone who might be hurting, sad or lonely.

Yes, we live in a world of turbulence and strife, but we can also create beauty in our own lives and bring it to the lives of others.

Being positive in a negative world.

That is true rebellion.

One of the first pictures you drew

of me and you. This, to me, is priceless.

On Considering The Value And Worth Of Things

We create our own fortunes by deciding what we value.

Value and worth are subjective.

They are up to each person.

Someone might say a painting by Van Gogh is priceless.

It's not.

It's worth whatever someone will pay for it.

And it's also worth whatever someone would be willing to sell it for.

As a child, you've asked me if I would ever sell your drawings to anyone for a billion dollars, and I've told you I wouldn't.

I wouldn't.

I'm being completely honest.

Because your drawings, what they mean to me, what they meant when you gave them to me, cannot be replaced by that artificial construct called money.

A billion dollars is only worth what we say it is.

It's only worth what other people agree it is worth, and what it can be traded for, whether that's houses or cars or whatever.

But to me, your drawings cannot be replaced, they are unique, they are priceless in value to me. I wouldn't sell them for a billion dollars, because no matter what I could buy with a billion dollars, it would never be as special, as worthy, as important, and valuable to me as those drawings you created for me.

Anyone with enough money could buy me a Ferrari or a boat or a mansion. But only you could create those drawings, only you could give them to me. And that, to me, is worth more than anything.

Don't let other people tell you what something is worth. Create your own worth for yourself.

People will say that it's important to have this car, or this house, or this stupid thing that will end up being thrown out and chucked into a landfill at some point.

But it isn't.

You can find happiness within yourself.

You don't need things.

We need to have food and shelter and heat and the necessities of life, yes, but beyond that, anything else is completely up to the person, it is completely subjective. Don't let anyone else brainwash you into thinking that something is valuable. Make that determination for yourself, and base value on what is truly priceless and important to you.

Whenever you're spending money, ask yourself if what you're spending it on is better or more useful than anything else you could possibly spend it on.

For a long time, I didn't spend money on myself or spend it on anyone other than you, or on paying our bills. Because for every $30 I might have spent on something else, I always asked myself if that thing would mean more to me than anything I could give to you with that $30. The answer was always no. You were and are always the most important person to me.

Some people will act as if having money creates worth in a person.

It doesn't.

As with things, worth is completely subjective. It's up to each person.

Someone's ability to think a certain way or to talk about incredible things or to have a fun and active imagination or a fantastic sense of humor is what is truly priceless. Finding someone who loves you for who you are, who makes you happy and who you enjoy spending time with, who really, truly loves you is priceless.

Don't judge people on if they have money or not. Sometimes people have worked hard for their money, other times they just got lucky and inherited it. They did nothing, they didn't work hard at all. They were just born and it was there. Some of the people working the hardest jobs hardly make anything and some of the people working the easiest jobs make millions.

Never confuse money with class, dignity or worth. Anyone can have money. They can inherit it through no work or effort of their own. They can be born into it, again through no work or effort of their own. They can win it in a lottery. They can get it through unscrupulous means.

But it takes an individual of distinct character to have class and dignity. And class and character take far more effort and self-worth to achieve. The poorest beggar can have more class and honor than the most gauche and vulgar billionaire.

Value the people and the things that make you happy.

Happiness is priceless.

The Gifts To Give Yourself Every Christmas And New Year

Something to think about every new year: What if at midnight you got amnesia? Suddenly you had no past with anyone. Looking around at the people in your life and how they treat you now, in the present, and in what you bring to each other's lives, and ONLY looking at that, with no sentiment or cling to the past, would you still want them around? It's an intriguing question...

Every year, I wish you a great Christmas and new year, happy memories, and good times. And I wish you all these gifts, to give yourself, for Christmas this year, and every year:

1.) Forgiveness. Let go of the past. You cannot change it. Forgive yourself your mistakes. Learn from them, avoid them in the future, but don't continue to condemn yourself for them.

2.) Hope. We've all been through bad times. But we've all been through good times too. If you look at your life, there are positives and negatives. Don't be afraid to be an optimist. Don't be afraid to think that the future is going to be terrific. Don't let the sadness of the past prevent you from embracing the happiness of the future.

3.) Happiness. When good things come into your life, when you meet people offering love and kindness and good, when you find situations that lift you up and offer great opportunities, then take them. They're gifts. Don't disregard or discard them, because you don't know when they'll arrive again. You deserve happiness. Always believe that.

4.) Belief. Believe in yourself. You have talents, you are beautiful, you are worthwhile, there is a reason for you in this world. Explore your talents and abilities. Realize that the people meant to be with you will find you beautiful, even your perceived flaws, and that perhaps oftentimes what you think to be a flaw is a treasure in another's eyes. Beauty is always in the eye of the beholder. Believe in your beauty, believe in your strength. To me, you are perfect. Others will find you the same. Trust me.

5.) Trust. Everyone makes mistakes. Everyone lies sometimes. But trust is about more than always speaking the truth. We often tell lies to spare the feelings of others, to cover our insecurities or vanities or to maintain civil relations with others in social and work situations. Base your trust not on words but actions. How does someone treat you? Are they there for you? Do they demonstrate they care for you and love you? Trust is ultimately about strength and security, and if someone is always there for you, if you can always count on them, if they're always sincerely displaying they care, then that's most important. Whether they say it or not. If their actions show they love you, that's what's important. Because when it comes down to it, anyone can talk, but it takes someone of character to back up their words with actions.

And always make your life a spectacular story and a wonderful adventure. This is all a ride, it's all a trip, so enjoy the journey . . .

On Being A Good Parent

Being a parent is the greatest responsibility you will ever have. You are responsible for bringing another human life to this planet. You are responsible for this being. When they are first born and for the first few years of their life, you are their lifeline, you are responsible for their care and their life. During that time and beyond it, you are that person's guardian, that person's champion, that person's guide and role model and best friend.

Be all those things. Do your best. Love. Open your heart. Love that being with all your heart.

Be the type of parent you would want to have.

Be a friend and confidante to your children, but realize they are children and you are an adult. You have the wisdom of many more years on your side, and it's up to you to guide them, to impart that wisdom to them and to help them on their journey. It's also up to you to teach them and prepare them for their own journey, because you won't always be with them, and you want them to be prepared, and protected, safe and smart and above all happy.

Talk to them.

Accept them.

Have open lines of communication with them.

Let them be themselves.

Be interested in their lives.

Love them no matter what.

Remember that they are humans, learning, taking this trip, trying to find their way, and help them do that, help them the way I have helped you, and tried to guide you, with advice like this.

But above all, love them, and let them know they are loved and accepted, and that they can be themselves, and that they have value and they are important and special. Because they are.

They are going to be different from you, because they are not you. They will develop their own tastes and interests and qualities, and that's wonderful. Take an interest and curiosity in those things so you can share those interests with them. As always, as long as they're not hurting themselves or other people, let them explore, let them find their likes and dislikes and do different things. Be beside them, watch over them, be there for them if and when they need you. But let them be themselves.

The greatest gift you can give them in that regard is love and acceptance.

Let them know that you will always love them, let them know that you accept them, let them know that they are important and their feelings and likes and preferences are important.

And remember that they are kids. They're going to like things that are different than what you like. They're going to like children's shows and books and music and games. They're going to be interested in things that kids are interested in. Go along with them, have fun with them.

Have fun. Enjoy the trip! Enjoy being a kid again with them!

Read to them from the time they are born. I started reading to you the day you got home from the hospital, two days after you were born, and I haven't stopped reading to you. Talk to them, converse, enrich their minds, tell them about science and art and music and people and you and your childhood and talk to them about all cool and fun things. And let them talk and listen to them.

I talk to you all the time. I have always talked to you, from the time before you were born. I used to talk to you when you were in your mother's belly, and talked to you every day since you were born. I'd talk to you about everything – the day-to-day adventures and travels of life – and you would talk to me as well. And I listened to you, because what you said, what you say, is important to me, because you are important to me.

Let your kids explore all different kinds of interests and hobbies and creative pursuits. Introduce them to all different kinds of foods and cultures and interesting things. Let them play different sports and participate with them. Coach their teams, show up to their games.

Anyone can buy someone an object.

But not everyone can spend meaningful time with someone.

And trust me, it means far more to your kids to spend time with them, to spend quality time, to show up for their events, to be there for them, than it will ever mean to just buy them things. Things come and go, memories can last forever, and time spent together is priceless.

It's up to a parent to help their child along the path, to hold their hand, to protect them, to show them how to be a good person.

Be a good example. Give them someone to emulate, someone to be proud of, someone who is a good example.

Be a good example in the person you are, and in the people you have around you. You need to make sure you surround yourself and your child with good people.

A person may not love themselves enough to think they deserve good people around them treating them right, but if they are a parent, they should love their children enough to know they deserve to be around good people treating them well.

The biggest question for any parent regarding the people you have around them, and in regard to the parent's own character is, would you want your child to end up with someone like them, or you, as a friend, a romantic partner or otherwise?

The answer should always be yes.

Always remember, time is the only thing that can only be spent once. You can only spend any moment once. Make sure you spend it on the right things. And spending that time with your children is always the best way to spend it. You will not regret that. You will not regret spending time with those people you love. Because you cannot ever repeat those moments again, you cannot recapture those moments again. No matter how much money you make, no matter how much stuff you accumulate, you will never be able to relive those moments again.

I was there when you said your first word, "DaDa."

I was there when you took your first step to me.

I was there for your first hit in baseball, and your first goal in soccer and your first drawings and songs and poems and smiles and laughs. I was there to play Thomas engines with you for countless hours, to play with cars and action figures and Legos, to play sports, to take walks and watch the giant machines at construction sites, and follow the garbage trucks to see the giant claws grab the garbage, and to go to children's events at the museums, and to go on your field trips, and see your school programs and so much more, and those are among the best memories of my life.

Those are priceless to me. You are priceless to me.

There is nothing more valuable than love.

Remember that when you have children, and cherish the love you share with them.

On Working Hard and Succeeding

It's rare anything is an instant success.

Usually success is the result of hard work and it's built on the foundation of failures overcome.

Sometimes the greatest victories are those all the sweeter for the effort put in to winning them.

Good luck follows good choices.

And luck itself is preparation meeting opportunity.

If you work hard, if you prepare, if you're ready for opportunity, you'll often be amazed at how "lucky" you will be when opportunity is drawn to you.

Practice, practice, practice. That is the only way to get better. Do things over and over and over again, keep learning better ways to do them, keep training in the best ways.

And always keep sight of your long-term goals.

Especially when you're tempted to take short cuts.

It might be tough to do the right thing in the short term, but it makes things easier in the long term. The difference between success and failure is often foresight and decisiveness

Every single day is a brand-new chance to start over... or another day to continue on the right path and be happy for the blessings it brings.

The journey of 1,000 miles doesn't begin with a single step. It begins with the thought and the conviction that you are going to take that step.

It's only through maximum velocity and unshakable faith in yourself that greatness can be achieved. If you're afraid to risk, if you're afraid to fail, you'll never succeed.

Never underestimate the power of discipline and perseverance.

The difference between those who accomplish things and those who talk for years about wanting to accomplish them, but who never do, is that the former know how to translate words into action and maintain their direction in doing so, regardless of the inevitable obstacles that come their way.

Consider the ramifications of your decisions. Every decision, big and small, sets you on a path. It sends you towards one thing and away from another.

Often, the larger the decision, the bigger the sacrifice of other options.

So, if you're going to choose one thing over another, be darn sure that the thing you're choosing is worth it, and will be in the long run.

You will have many dreams. You will pursue many things. But whatever you do, do your best. It's ok to change directions if you change interests or want to do something else. I've let you try many different things growing up. You did basketball for a few seasons, you did tae kwon do for a few months, but you decided they weren't for you. That's fine. Find the things that are right for you. You decided you wanted to devote more time to soccer, and of course I let you follow that passion. But while you were doing those other sports, I was proud that you gave them your best effort.

Whatever you do, put your heart into it and give it your best effort.

Work hard, be smart, don't be afraid to try new things or change directions if things aren't working.

Adaptability and flexibility are important too, and sometimes you have to try a lot of different paths before you find the one that works for you.

Work towards your passions and your interests.

If you are passionate about what you do, if you put your all into something you love, then work won't seem like drudgery, it will be fun, it will be a challenge that intrigues and interests you, it will be an adventure.

And when you succeed, be humble, be a good sport, be proud of yourself, be happy and know that your Dad is very proud of you and happy for you.

You can do it!

I believe in you!

Pursue your dreams!

On Surrounding Yourself With Good People

The primary way you can really learn if you can trust someone is by trusting them.

The other way is by observing how trustworthy they are and seeing how they treat others.

Listen. Observe. People will show you who they are if you just pay attention. Then you can see if they're good people to have in your life.

Do they make you happy?

Do they make you laugh?

Do they make you feel comfortable?

Do they accept you as you are?

Do they make good decisions, are they positive, do they encourage you to make good decisions and be positive?

Do they encourage you without being jealous? Are they happy for your successes?

Are they happy with their own efforts and successes and encouraging of others?

It's important to be around good people. It will make your life easier, better and happier.

Your worth does not diminish based upon others' inability to recognize and appreciate it. You don't need someone to validate you. But everyone likes company, everyone likes to have people around to share the trip with, so make sure you surround yourself with cool, fun, nice, good, solid people who will make your life better for them being in it.

If you surround yourself with positive, optimistic, high-achieving people, you're going to find yourself more optimistic and driven. If you surround yourself with negative, pessimistic people of low aspirations, you're going to find yourself feeling bogged down.

Do not let the jerks get you down, because they're always going to be too lazy and pathetic to build themselves up. And don't let positive people go, because they are way too rare in this world. Always take the path of greatest happiness and achievement and you'll never regret it.

Don't ever judge someone on anything they can't help or anything out of their control.

Don't judge someone on their hair or eye color, or the color of their skin, or their race, or their gender or their orientation, who they love or who they like, or whether they were born rich or poor.

Consider them on the decisions they've made and the things they can control.

Are they good to other people? Are they good to people they really don't need anything from?

You know who your real friends are if all you have to offer them is your friendship and they are still by your side.

It's telling if a person is rude to waiters or waitresses or people who work at a fast food drive thru. They don't need to be, and there's no reason to be. If someone is a jerk to others for no reason, there's a good chance they'll be a jerk to you for no reason at some point. Don't be that person. Respect others. Be polite. Treat other people the way you would like them to treat you.

Remember the people who are with you when you're down. They're the only ones who deserve to be with you when you're up.

People will show you who they are, if you let them, and you have the patience to observe. The question is, do you want to see people as they really are, or do you want to see them as you want them to be, using the shorthand of what they reveal with your imagination and desires for what you wish them to be filling the gaps?

You want to see people as they really are.

You want them to see you as you really are.

That's the only way you can find your true friends. That's the only way you can really trust people.

Always make sure you have plenty of smart, funny, creative people in your life. You'll never want for surprises.

Age is absolutely no factor in wisdom or maturity. Two people the same age with the same problems can and will act differently regarding them, in good and bad ways. You can never tell.

React to people's actions and intentions, not your preconceived notions of them based upon societal boxes.

Don't be a relativist when it comes to people treating you poorly. The friend or romantic partner who has ONLY backstabbed you a few times or ONLY treats you terribly once a week may be better than the one who treats you horribly more often, but they're still bad. They're still worse than the clear majority of people out there who wouldn't treat you horribly at all. Don't sell yourself short.

Yes, there are good people out there. But your odds of finding them aren't good if you're always hanging around with bad people.

Every moment you spend with someone is a moment you can't spend with someone else.

So why spend it on someone who isn't best for you?

Why not get that person out of your life, so that you're open to find someone better?

Like attracts like.

If you surround yourself with positive people, if you are a positive person, you are more likely to attract positive people into your life.

And you never, ever want to surround yourself with negative people.

Or spend more time with negative people than you ever need to spend.

Leave. Get them out of your life. Move on.

All it takes is one jerky kid to wreck a playground and one jerky kid leaving to make it infinitely better. Same thing could be said of adults.

The weak hide behind anger and negativity, slaves to the opinions of others. The strong are confident they can overcome anything and aren't afraid to be positive, caring, and good.

The more you surround yourself with good people and eliminate the jerks, the happier your life is going to be.

It's good to be generous, it's admirable to give, but recognize when you're being taken.

Yes, there are times in every relationship -- family, friend, romantic partner -- when the scales tip decisively in one direction and there's more take than give. During illness and hardship, it's important to be there for the people you love and to stand by them. This comment is not about those times. This comment is about the give-and-take of everyday life.

If someone consistently takes more than they give, if they consistently are dragging you down and being negative, you need to move on and find a more positive place and more positive people to be around. They are out there. Trust me. We live in a world of billions and billions of people. I have met thousands and thousands of people in my life. There are good people out there. You just need to persevere and find them. But you can't find them if you're wasting your time spending time with negative people, especially those that drain your energy and drag you down.

You deserve happiness.

You deserve to have a great life.

You deserve people who love you and appreciate you.

Somewhere, their hearts are longing to find you. Open yourself up to that, open yourself up to the possibility of finding them. You will. And you'll be thankful and happy you did.

And always remember, you'll always have your family and closest friends. I'll always be there for you. I'll always be your friend.

On Being A Friend
And Choosing Good Friends

    Surround yourself with people with whom you have things in common and who make you feel good when you're around them.

    People who you enjoy talking to, who you can talk to, who you can trust.

    People who make you laugh, who make you happy.

    People who are there for you when you're sad or when times are tough.

    People who you feel connected to, who you feel really accept you and make you stronger, who encourage you to be your best and who love you at your best or worst but always want you to be at your best and want you to be happy.

And who, above all, just want to be with you, who just want your companionship, and whose companionship is all you want from them.

A friend is someone who is with you when you have nothing to offer them but your friendship.

Your friends are the people who are there for you when they have nothing to gain from you but your friendship.

There are also people you might meet who are going to try to control you with their advice. People who don't really have your best interests in mind, but their own. They're trying to manipulate or control you, or they feel uncomfortable with you. Maybe they're jealous. Maybe they're insecure. Maybe they're not strong enough to stand on their own and they're afraid if you do, you won't want to be with them or around them.

And maybe there's good reason you shouldn't be with them or around them. One good reason is if they're trying to make you feel bad for being yourself and just trying to be happy.

Negative people like to congregate with each other because they make one another look and feel better about their own diminished lives.

Likewise, good people and achievers tend to be drawn to each other because they can associate and share progress without feeling any resentment from those who aren't on their level. If you want to achieve your goals, if you want to elevate your own life, stay away from the negative people, and follow the paths of the achievers.

It's always better to be hated for what you are than loved for what you are not.

Friends are people who make your life better for being in it. If they don't, and what's more, if they consistently make your life the worse for being a part of it, they're not worth having in your life. There are over six billion people in this world. You can and will find better friends. You don't need anyone who brings you down and isn't worthy of you -- or even more important, who isn't worthy of the person you want to be.

The same goes for the person with whom you're in a relationship. They should make you a better person for them being in your life, and you should do the same.

On Romantic Relationships

When I was a kid, my grandfather, your great-grandfather, used to cook dinner for us from time to time. As he was a former officer in the Air Force, his manner was rather brusque, and his repertoire in the kitchen was rather limited.

One of the favorite things he liked to prepare was corned beef hash.

My siblings and I were not huge fans of corned beef hash. But he would always try to persuade us by saying "You like corned beef? You like potatoes? Then you like corned beef hash!"

My reply was usually something to the line of that I liked pizza and I liked ice cream, but I didn't like pizza and ice cream together.

And that's kind of how you should look at romantic relationships. Sometimes things are great separately, and sometimes those things go great together, and sometimes they do not.

You are an awesome person. You might meet an awesome girl you're interested in. But you might not be compatible in a romantic relationship. That doesn't mean you're bad or she's bad, it might mean you want or need different things or you just might not have a lot in common or your personalities might be incompatible.

On the other hand, you might both be awesome and you might go together brilliantly. Like, er, um, some good corned beef hash! (Somewhere, your great-grandfather is laughing.)

Either way, try to always have fun in romantic partnerships. Make sure you choose good people to be with, who make your life better for them being in it, and try to be a person who makes the other person's life better as well.

When you are young, particularly, and just dating as a pre-teen and teen and even into your twenties, don't worry about the whole concept of marriage and being together forever and all that. That's a prescribed notion pressed upon us by society. If you're happy with the person, stay with them. If you're not, move on. If you remain happy with the person and you're with them for a long time and you both want to make it official by getting married (after you're in your mid-twenties at least, of course, because you'll want some time for both of you to grow together and experience the world), then go ahead and do it. But only after really getting to know that person and really being sure that that person is the right one for you.

Don't ever, ever, ever, ever feel like you HAVE to be in a relationship.

Society and particularly entertainment are constantly brainwashing people into thinking they HAVE TO be in a relationship. Movies and TV shows and books and entertainment are always driven towards people meeting and falling in love and being together. And do you want to know why? Because they need to amp up the drama to keep people watching! And the way to do that is by having people get together and break up and make up and everything else. The more action they have going on, the more people are going to tune in to see what happens. But real life isn't like that. When that happens in real life – the constant breaking up and making up, the never-ending drama – it gets really tiresome really fast and it's just a waste of your time and life.

You don't HAVE TO be with someone. And in fact, you can be very happy being by yourself. And in fact, you can be much, much, much happier alone than you will be if you're with the wrong person.

Think of romantic partnerships like spice in a food – you can eat the food without spice and it might be perfectly delicious, you can add the spice and it might make that food even better, but if you add the wrong spice, it will make the food worse.

Eventually, everyone pursues romantic partnerships, but that doesn't mean you always have to be in a romantic partnership. Neither does anyone else. As with any partnership, you should only be with people, you should only have people in your life, if they make your life better than it would be without them there.

What do you look for in a romantic partner?

Someone who makes you happy as much as possible, because life's too short and your time is too important to be with someone who makes you unhappy.

Someone who makes you proud of yourself and your actions when you're with them.

Someone who you're proud to be with.

Someone who brings out your best, but stands by you at your worst.

Someone who challenges you in good ways.

Someone who you can laugh and have fun with, who you can be serious with sometimes, and who you just like. You should love them, yes, but you should also LIKE them.

Always remember, you don't have to be with anyone to be happy or complete. You can be happy all by yourself. So, choose carefully, and pick someone who is going to add to your life, who is going to make it a better place far more often than not.

Every relationship you are in should aid in your POSITIVE evolution. Otherwise you're better off alone and standing still or evolving yourself rather than being with someone who's going to set you back.

There are going to be people you're attracted to, and there are people you won't be attracted to.

There are going to be people that you are inexplicably attracted to – you feel drawn to them, compelled to be around them, like an invisible force, even if you may not like them or think they're good for you.

Trust me, I've been there. It's happened to me. I've been in those situations.

Listen to your brain in those situations. Don't fall prey to an attraction to someone that doesn't make your life better. Because that attraction isn't worth being miserable. There are over six billion people on this planet. There are other people out there who you will feel that attraction to who will also be good people who will make your life better. Hold out for one of them. They'll come along, don't worry!

Appreciate the good ones. The loyal. The consistent. The steadfast. The reliable. The ones who are always there, that you always know will be there without question.

Because all too often we don't. We live in a society that celebrates the dramatic, the erratic, the inconsistent and the unreliable and we romanticize their affection as a wonderful surprise when it arrives. But there's something to be said for the people who just make every day a small gift with their constant presence.

There are going to be people that you like but aren't attracted to, and they may be attracted to you. Be respectful of their feelings and your own. Don't feel forced to be with them as anything other than what you want to be. If you just want to be friends, that's fine. If they're really your friend, if they really do care about you, they'll respect that.

And vice versa. If someone says they only like you as a friend, respect that. There are probably a lot of good qualities you appreciate about that person and if they're a good person, wouldn't you want them to still be in your life? Of course. Respect their feelings.

The same goes for breakups.

You are going to have your heart broken. We have all had our hearts broken.

You are going to break someone's heart. Again, we have all broken others' hearts.

Just always try to be respectful.

There are a lot of different reasons for breakups. Not all of them are huge and dramatic. Sometimes you just grow and evolve in different directions. People move. People go away to college. People change. We all meet people at different times in their lives, and when they change and we change, we either continue to fall in love with the people each other becomes or we grow apart. That's perfectly normal. It can be sad, yes, when we break up with someone, but that doesn't always mean they're bad or we're bad, sometimes it just means we're going on separate paths moving forward.

Be thankful for the time you've spent together.

Be thankful for how you've made each other's lives better and more fun to live in while you've been together.

Look at your mother and I. We split up. We are not together. But we had a lot of good times when we were together and most importantly, we had you! We created you. We created this wonderful, amazing, cool person and that makes the time she and I spent together worth it. We both made our lives better for being together because we both have you in our lives because we were together.

So, if things don't work out, move on, and wish that person the best going forward. There's nothing wrong with wishing someone happiness and good with their lives whether they're with you or not. In fact, we should do that, especially if they helped us have happier lives and if we really care about them, we want to see them happy whether they're with us or not.

Just because you don't spend the rest of your life with someone doesn't mean the time you spent with them wasn't worthwhile.

Always make sure you try to make someone's life better than it was when you arrived in it.

Now, that may not always be the case on the other side. Sometimes people will not be cool when you break up. Especially if they're being negative or not bringing something good to your life and you decide to break up with them and move on. They may not like that, for whatever reason. Sometimes they will act poorly. If that's the case, just move on.

Ultimately it is your decision.

You have a right to that decision.

And if it's your decision to break up, you have the right to take that action. Don't feel guilty.

Don't let yourself be made to feel guilty. Stand behind your decision.

Don't engage in arguing, don't engage in negative behavior, stand up for yourself as needed and move on and away from that person. If they are being negative, if they are being mean to you or trying to make you feel bad, do not engage them, do not have them as part of your life at all, cut them off and leave them behind and don't look back. Don't ever bring someone back into your life after they have been needlessly mean or harmful to you. If someone cannot show you respect, then they don't deserve to have you in their lives.

Don't go out of your way to be a jerk to them, stand up for yourself, stand by your decision, move on and ignore them and do your own thing. You'll find better people to spend your time with, and it'll always be for the best.

Sometimes that happens. Sometimes people seem too good to be true because they're lying or pretending to be someone they aren't. But the lies always come to the surface and eventually everyone shows their true colors. Again, just move on.

That said, be open to trust other people. Not that same person who treated you badly, you don't want to go back to them if they've done that, but others. Don't blame someone new for the behavior of your ex. Because they're not that person. Everyone is unique. Every person you're in a relationship with deserves a chance, deserves trust, deserves to be treated on their own behavior and merits. You can't blame them for the behavior of someone else, and they can't blame you for the behavior of someone else either. Go into each dating experience or relationship with open eyes and an open heart.

Because surprises aren't always bad. And there are good people in the world too.

Sometimes things aren't too good to be true, they're just good and true.

Look at how that person treats you. Look at how they treat other people. Look at how they treat the world, how they look at the world. Are they a good person? Are they kind? Are they caring and compassionate? Are they positive? Do they have a good sense of humor?

Those are all important things.

Those are all good things to look for in a partner.

There are certain things you will wish for from time to time in a person – a certain style or personality or whatever – but always go beyond those details and try to find someone who is good at heart, who is respectful and kind.

What you want and the kind of person you want may and probably will change over the years. Remembering where you were and what you once wished for is key in appreciating how far you've come and what you now have.

Don't let anyone manipulate you. It happens sometimes. It can happen to anyone. So don't feel bad if you get manipulated, but once you're aware of it, get out of the situation and move on.

Again, there are over six billion people on this planet. You will find other romantic partners. There are people out there who will treat you well, who will love you as you are, and who will treat you with respect.

But you'll never find them if you're wasting your time with someone who doesn't treat you well or doesn't treat you with respect.

Don't waste your time.

It's better to be alone and open to find those cool people than to be tied up with the wrong one.

If anyone ever says to you "If you really loved me, you'd do this..." say "If you really loved me, you wouldn't try to force me into doing something I don't want to do."

Someday, someone is going to break your heart. It will tear you apart. It will make you feel awful. But somehow, somehow, try to retain the thought that this, too, is a positive thing. You're not meant to be with them if they don't want to be with you. And by leaving you, they're giving you an important gift – the freedom to potentially find the person with whom you ARE meant to be.

When you're going out on a date, remember these things: Be nice, be polite, be yourself. Always be respectful to people. And always be yourself, because if anyone is going to fall in love with you, you want them to fall in love with the person you are, inside.

When it comes to choosing a romantic partner, don't underestimate the power of peace and comfort. Find someone with whom you feel comfortable, with whom you can be yourself, who will accept you as you are, and who you can just enjoy a calm, comfortable existence. The world is full of enough drama and unpredictability and turmoil, the less you have in your home with your spouse or significant other, the better.

Most of life is just hanging out. So, if you want to be with someone, pick someone you feel comfortable and can have fun just hanging out with.

Make sure you're with someone who makes you laugh. A lot. Someone who makes you smile. A lot. Someone who always makes you feel like you matter, like you're important, like you're special, because you are!

Don't worry about labels. Boyfriend, girlfriend, married, in a relationship, whatever.

Just be together.

It takes a while to eschew the security of labels, until you realize labels hold no security.

Everything from wedding vows on down has been broken and discarded by people at one time or another. The only way to know if something is sure and true is if you both realize your life would be profoundly diminished due to the absence of the other, and that there's no one with whom you could imagine spending your time and having as much joy and love in your life.

Forget pretending to be someone else and enticing someone to fall in love with an illusion that will become a gilded cage.

Be yourself and you'll end up with someone whose uniqueness is a complement to yours and who can truly say they love YOU rather than the illusion they've been tricked to believe is you.

It's rare that a relationship will be completely equal in regards to give and take. But whenever you start to get over the 60-40 range, be wary.

And if you stray into 70-30, think very seriously about whether that 30 you get is truly worth the 70 you're losing.

It's not ``mean" or ``selfish" to retain some self-worth and expect appreciation and reciprocation.

You are a valuable person. You are an important person. You are worthwhile.

Don't forget that, or allow anyone to convince you otherwise.

Never settle. Look for, strive for, and accept no less than the love you deserve. Because while you're settling for "ok" or "good for now" or "best you think you can get," you might miss your chance to find and be with someone amazing a lot sooner rather than later.

You are an amazing person.

You deserve to be with an amazing person.

You both deserve to be with someone who recognizes the beauty and awesomeness of each other.

We're all a little crazy, we've all got the fireworks of insanity bursting within us. The key is finding someone for whom those uncontrollable bursts of our being fill their eyes with beauty, their hearts with fire and their quickened breath with one sustained smile in a word: Wow.

On Growing And Evolving

Life isn't about finding yourself, it's about creating yourself.

Take a picture of yourself tonight. Look at it tomorrow. That's the only person you're competing against. Be a better person every day.

For the first 15 minutes you're awake in the morning, think about nothing but the good things in your life, and see how much it changes your life for the better. Stay positive, keep moving forward.

If you string together enough of a good present, it becomes a good future.

Sometimes what you need to be happy changes without you realizing it. And the reason you find yourself unhappy isn't because you haven't achieved what you wanted, it's because you're chasing after something you don't need anymore.

Make sure you're moving towards the things you really want and need, the things that really make you happy. Be honest with yourself. You know yourself better than anyone.

If you always try to do the right thing and give your best effort, regardless of the outcome, you tend to have few regrets.

Always keep an open mind, until you need to close it.

Your imagination is one of the most valuable treasures you will ever have.

Read. Explore. Try new things. This is an incredible world, full of a wide array of people and foods and culture and beauty that are waiting to be explored. See as much as you can, explore as much as you can. Meet different people, talk about interesting things, spend your time wisely on things that will expand your mind and imagination and will make your heart sing. Find your new favorite songs, favorite foods, favorite places, favorite people. Take it all in, be present, look around, notice little things, little details, wonderful aspects of everything.

Create magnificent memories.

That's what life is about.

Be happy. Follow your bliss.

Be a part of this beautiful world and enjoy the trip!

Sometimes things aren't too good to be true, they're just good and true.

Sometimes the universe conspires in such a strange and beautiful way that all you can or want to do is happily bask in hope and gratitude. Don't mistrust it. The more you do, the less magic you allow into your life.

Really, when it comes down to it, you either see your life as a miracle or an accident. You won't find out whether you're correct until you pass from this world into whatever comes next, but your answer will go a long way in determining your happiness while you're here on earth.

Believe in goodness.

Believe in your ability to find it and have positive and great things in your life.

Believe in yourself.

Believe in happiness.

Move confidently towards your future.

Be confident and curious and evolve and travel and explore in a life of happiness.

Never Forget . . .

I love you.

You will always be the greatest person I have ever met, the most amazing human being I have ever had the proud honor of meeting. You're my best friend.

I am so happy for all the awesome times and memories we have shared together.

But the great thing about happy memories is that you can always make more, and I look forward to all the great memories we will have.

No matter what you do or where you go I'll always be thinking of you. No matter how old you get, I'll always remember you as the tiny blessing you were the day you were born. And no matter what, I'll always love you.

We are all time travelers. We just travel a second at a time.

Take in the view, revel in every moment, have fun, laugh, love, feel, notice the details.

We are all time travelers.

We just travel a second at a time.

Revel in every second, because you are a blessing to me, and this world.

And as always, enjoy the trip . . .

I love you.

Dad

Other books by Sean Leary

The Arimathean (novel / fantasy)

The Blood of Destiny (novel / fantasy)

Black Knight Apocalypse (novel / sci-fi)

Luna Death Trigger (novel / sci-fi)

Does The Shed Skin Know It Was Once A Snake? (short stories)

Every Number Is Lucky To Someone (short stories)

My Life As A Freak Magnet (short stories)

Exorcising Ghosts (graphic novel)

Here Comes The Goot! (children's/beginning readers)

Go, Racecars, Go! (children's/beginning readers)

Nine Little Penguin Ninjas

(children's/beginning readers)

Baby Bird

(children's/beginning readers)

We Are All Characters

(children's/beginning readers)

Beautiful Remnants of Chaotic Failures

(poetry)

Danger Maps

(poetry)

Every Broken Heart Creates The Pieces That Will Pave The Way To The Place Your Heart Will Call Home

(poetry)

Tricks of the Light

(poetry)

The Soft Venom of Promise

(poetry)

The Night Universal
(poetry)

There Is Truth In The Untamed Beat of a Heart
(poetry)

We Are Shadows In The Absence of Light
(poetry)

Magnets & Mysteries, Soft Curves & Comets
(poetry)

Infinite Sky
(poetry)

Sean Leary's Greatest Hits, volume one
(humor)

Sean Leary's Greatest Hits, volume two
(humor)

Sean Leary's Greatest Hits, volume three
(humor)

Your Favorite Band
(stageplay / screenplay)

Dingo Boogaloo

(stageplay / screenplay)

Rock City Live!

(stageplay / screenplay)

My Life As A Freak Magnet: The Stageplay

(stageplay)

Shots 2 The Heart: Shot One

(stageplay)

Shots 2 The Heart: Shot Two

(stageplay)

This Is The Best Worst Idea I Ever Had

(short stories)

The I Can't Even Adult Coloring Book

(coloring book)

For more writing and more information,

see seanleary.com.

www.ingramcontent.com/pod-product-compliance
Lightning Source LLC
Chambersburg PA
CBHW032116090426
42743CB00007B/366